Eagles for Kids

by Charlene Gieck
photography by Tom and Pat Leeson

NORTHWORD PRESS

Minnetonka, Minnesota

WILDLIFE *for Kids* **SERIES** ™

NorthWord Press
5900 Green Oak Drive
Minnetonka, MN 55343
1-800-328-3895

National Wildlife Federation® is the nation's largest conservation, education and advocacy organization. Since 1936, NWF has educated people from all walks of life to protect nature, wildlife and the world we all share.

Ranger Rick® is an exciting magazine published monthly by National Wildlife Federation® about wildlife, nature and the environment for kids ages 7 to 12. For more information about how to subscribe to this magazine, write: National Wildlife Federation, 8925 Leesburg Pike, Vienna, Virginia 22184.

NWF's World Wide Web Site www.nwf.org provides instant computer access to information about National Wildlife Federation, conservation issues and ideas for getting involved in protecting our world.

Designed by Origins Design, Inc.

ISBN 1-55971-133-7

Printed in Malaysia

But you never were made, as I,
On the wings of the wind to fly!
The eagle said.

– Will Carleton

We all know the bald eagle. It's the national symbol of the United States. The eagle usually makes us think of things like strength, dignity, and freedom. These images inspired America's leaders to place the bald eagle on the country's Great Seal in 1782. Since then, the bald eagle has been a common feature on posters, business signs, and even money.

*We usually think of strength, dignity, and
freedom when looking at an eagle.*

For centuries, Native Americans have admired the bald eagle. The eagle was often carved at the very top of totem poles, the place of highest respect. Because eagles are able to soar high into the sky and disappear from sight, the Pueblo people believed the eagle was related to the Sun. They prized eagle feathers, believing the feathers would carry their prayers to the heavens. Eagle feathers are still used today in tribal religious rites or are awarded to persons performing deeds of great valor.

The eagle is honored by Native Americans in the eagle dance, which is still performed at many powwows today.

The bald eagle's tail has twelve white feathers, each measuring from eleven to sixteen inches in length.

The dignified image of the bald eagle comes partly from its coloration—a pure white head and tail contrasted with a dark brown body. It's almost as if they are dressed for a formal event. This coloration makes them easy to identify.

Eagles don't get those white feathers right away. During the first four to five years of life, an eagle's feathers are dark brown, including those on the head and tail. These brown eagles are called "immatures." Immatures often have white

feathers under their wings and on their chests. The amount of white varies with each eagle. Young immature eagles are often confused with golden eagles and hawks. By five years of age all bald eagles have the white head and tail. They are now ready to breed and have their own family.

If the bald eagle has feathers on its head, then why is it called bald? The name comes from an Old English word, "balde," which means "white." So it was natural to call this pure white-headed bird the bald eagle.

Their large size and the fierce look in their eyes give eagles the appearance of strength. The bald eagle has a wingspan of seven to eight feet. Try spreading your arms to your sides and have someone measure your "wingspan." Are you bigger than an eagle?

Female eagles are about forty inches tall. They are larger than male eagles, which measure about thirty inches tall. Even though eagles appear to be huge, they are not very heavy. They weigh only eight to fourteen pounds. Their large appearance comes from many layers of feathers. Like most other birds, they have hollow bones that make them lightweight for flying. Struts or braces inside the hollow bones keep the bones from breaking easily.

A seven-foot wingspan can make it difficult to get into the air. Once in flight, though, the long broad wings are ideal for hours of soaring over the countryside. Eagles use moving air currents to make travel effortless and quick. During a good journey, they will seldom flap their wings.

Eagles often take flight from a perch in a tall tree.

Eagles are "birds of prey," which means they eat meat. Fish is the favorite food of bald eagles. The birds are not fussy eaters and will eat most types of fish, caught alive or found dead. They eat many animals besides fish, including geese, ducks, rabbits, turtles, and other small animals. They also eat carrion, which is the decaying flesh of dead animals. Carrion is especially important in winter when other foods are not easy to find.

This immature bald eagle is feeding on a salmon, which is one of a bald eagle's favorite kinds of fish.

To catch fish, eagles watch the water surface from a perch or while soaring in the air. Then they swoop down and drop their feet right in the water to catch the fish. Many times they miss their target and have to try again and again.

Eagles often steal food from other eagles or from other birds of prey such as ospreys. Eagles are opportunistic feeders, eating almost anything that is available. Well, almost anything . . . the one thing they don't like eating is vegetables!

Eagles fly at high speed to take their prey
by surprise when they swoop down.

You might be called "eagle-eyed" if you have good vision and notice things quickly. Eagles have excellent eyesight. They can see six to eight times better than people. An eagle can see a rabbit two miles away! You would need a good pair of binoculars to see that well. Good eyesight is very important to an eagle soaring high over a lake looking for lunch.

The talons, or claws, on an eagle's toes are curved and razor-sharp for catching and holding their prey. This gives eagles the name raptor, which comes from a Latin word "rapere," meaning to grip or grasp. Rough bumps on the eagle's toes also help them hold slippery, wiggling fish. A raptor's feet are important to capturing food and also as a method of protection. The long talons and vise-like grip can inflict serious wounds to intruders.

Bald eagle feet have no feathers on them. Three of the toes point forward and one points back, for the best grip.

Male and female eagles usually spend most of the winter apart. When they find each other again in late winter, they perform courtship displays including "cartwheels" in mid-air. The display starts when one bird flips on its back in the air and grasps the talons of the other bird.

Together the two birds spiral down through the air like a cartwheel. Just when you think they will crash into the ground, they separate. Then they fly back up into the air to continue courtship. This activity is thought to bond the birds to each other.

Nest building begins shortly after courtship. Gathering sticks for the nest takes a long time, and both birds help. The nest, or aerie, is a large stick structure. When it's first built, a nest may measure three feet wide by three feet deep. Pine branches or grasses line the nest, making a soft layer for the young eagles.

Eagles choose their nest site carefully. They prefer a tall tree in a quiet area near food and water.

This scientist is measuring the size of a nest—with eaglets in it!

If the pair nested together before, they will probably use their old nest again. Since more sticks will be added, nests get larger each year. The largest nest ever found was in Ohio. It was nearly nine feet wide and twelve feet deep. It was probably bigger than your bedroom. Most nests are as big as your bed.

The area around the pair's nest is called a territory. It is fiercely defended from intruders. Other eagles and birds are driven out of the area by the pair of nesting eagles.

The female on the left is slightly bigger than the male on the right.

Eagles need several things for nesting: a large tree, a source of food, and peace and quiet. They usually nest near rivers or lakes so they can be close to sources of fish. The nest tree will usually be a living pine tree, but aspen, oak, cottonwood, and other trees are used too. The tree they choose will always be the one that towers above other trees around it. Since eagles like to be able to see what's around them, the nest is built near the top of the tree.

One adult usually stays near the nest when the young are small, while the other adult hunts for food.

Each egg is laid about two days apart in the nest.

One to three eggs are laid in early spring. Eagle eggs are plain white and close in size to a goose egg. The female sits on, or incubates, the eggs for 35-40 days. The male also incubates the eggs or brings food to his mate. He can often be seen perching close by, keeping a watchful eye for trouble.

When the eggs hatch, the emerging tiny eaglets are covered with thick down. These special fluffy feathers keep the eaglets warm until their regular feathers develop. The eaglets are helpless, unable to walk or stand up.

One or two young is the average per nest—never more than three are born.

Pages 26-27: This young eaglet was the first to hatch. There may be more in the large nest.

The adults are now kept very busy finding food for these always hungry babies. The female eagle carefully tears the meat into small pieces and puts it into the eaglets' mouths. Eaglets grow quickly and are soon able to move around in the nest and start grabbing at food as soon as it arrives.

Eaglets look very different from their parents, but they grow and change quickly.

Pages 30-31: Adults are kept very busy finding food for their hungry young eaglet.

These eaglets have begun growing their first brown feathers, which will replace their fluffy brown down.

When they are about three weeks old, the chicks start growing dark brown feathers. Most of the eaglets' time is spent eating, sleeping, caring for their feathers, and exercising their tiny wings. By three months of age, the eaglets are ready for fledging, or taking their first flight. Sometimes the first flight is by accident. They may be knocked out of the nest by the wind when they're on the edge of the nest.

If they are lucky, they will flutter to a nearby perch and later fly back to the nest. If they are unlucky, they can end up on the ground. The adults may not care for them if they cannot see them in the grass and brush under the tree. Some will die because they cannot return to the nest on their own.

This adult bald eagle is calling out a warning to another eagle in the area—stay away!

Young eagles stay with the adults for approximately eight weeks after leaving the nest. The young soon learn to hunt for their own food.

As late fall approaches, young eagles start moving southward. They have now learned how to hunt and to take care of themselves. These eagles, now called immatures, leave the nest area before the adults.

Records show that some nest sites have been used for over thirty years. Eagles that survive the difficult first years of life can live to be up to forty years old.

These immatures will soon fledge and begin hunting on their own.

Bald eagles are found only in North America. At one time they nested along rivers and lakes throughout Canada and the United States, except Hawaii, where they have never nested. Eagles can still be found in many states, especially Minnesota, Wisconsin, Michigan, Washington, Oregon, and Florida. They are also located in much of Alaska and Canada.

Nesting sites are near forested lakes and rivers in areas with little disturbance. Eagles do not like to nest near humans. The sight of an approaching person can cause the adult birds to leave the nest. When this happens, the eggs or young may become chilled and die. If you are hiking or boating, stay away from eagle nests. Only watch them from a distance. Use binoculars instead of trying to get too close.

Not all nests are in trees, as this eagle in Alaska shows us.

Eagles migrate each spring and fall. Adults will also travel south in the winter if the northern rivers and lakes freeze over. Large groups of eagles can be found near dams on major rivers where the moving water does not freeze. The Mississippi River is a very important waterway for bald eagles. Wildlife refuges in many states offer protection for wintering eagles.

Winter is a great time to watch eagles. You can watch them from your car, which acts as a hiding place. Watching from your car lets you enjoy this activity from a warm spot, too. Many states along the Mississippi River now hold special eagle-watching events. Many people are learning a lot about eagles.

In winter, as in summer, eagles often call to each other to let them know they are nearby.

Approximately sixty species of eagles live in the world. There are four types of eagles—sea eagles, booted eagles, buteonine eagles, and serpent eagles.

Sea Eagles: The bald eagle is part of this group. Sea eagles are found nearly worldwide along wooded seacoasts, lakes, and rivers. They are not present in South America. They have combinations of dark and white feathers. They have short, bare legs and toes with long, sharp talons. They feed primarily on fish, but will eat waterfowl, mammals, turtles, and carrion. Sea eagles have long, broad wings and short, wedge-shaped tails. Their large nests are made of sticks and built in tall trees.

An eagle's beak is about three inches long. It is very strong for ripping apart food.

Booted Eagles: The golden eagle belongs in this group. Booted eagles live on wooded and barren mountains throughout Europe and Asia and in northern Africa and western North America. Most are dark brown in color; the golden eagle has golden feathers on its head and on the back of its neck. Booted eagles feed on rabbits, rodents, snakes, birds, and carrion. They are called "booted" because they have feathers down to their toes. Their nests are usually found on the ledges of rocky cliff faces.

Buteonine Eagles: These, including the harpy eagle, are the largest and most powerful of eagles. They live in dense, tropical jungles of Mexico, the Philippines, and South America. Buteonine eagles have crested heads, giving them a witchlike appearance. Their short, broad wings make them able to move around in thick jungles. Their diet includes birds and tree-dwelling mammals like monkeys. Their nests are built in trees.

Serpent Eagles: The bateleur eagle is a well-known representative of this group. Serpent eagles are found in the tropical grasslands of Africa, Europe, Asia, and Australia. They have short tails compared to other eagles. Their short, bare legs are covered with rough scales. The toes are strong and short. They eat snakes, insects, fish, mammals, and birds. Their nests are found in tall broad-topped trees.

Eagles were once endangered. At one time we feared that this great bird would disappear forever. The number of eagles dropped quickly in the early 1950s and 1960s. DDT, a powerful and long-lasting poison, was used to protect crops from insects after World War II. Unfortunately, fish and birds began dying after eating insects treated with DDT.

DDT caused eagles to lay thin-shelled eggs. The eggs broke under the weight of female eagles as they tried to incubate the eggs. The number of eagles declined when no young were produced for many years. The United States banned DDT in 1972, and eagle populations have been growing slowly ever since. They are no longer endangered. But eagles have other problems, including shooting, trapping, disease, and collisions with utility poles or vehicles. Eagles don't have as many nest trees as they used to have either. Many of the tall trees have been cut down for lumber. Lakeshores have too often become places for homes and businesses. And many lakes have become too busy with boaters and fishermen. Eagles need solitude.

Bald eagles have excellent eyesight. They have been known to spot another eagle flying as far away as fifteen miles.

*By banding eaglets, biologists can
study their movement and habits.*

We know a great deal about eagles now. Nest locations in
most states are put on maps and checked each year. Young
eagles are often banded with small aluminum leg bands.
The band has a unique number that identifies the eagle for
life. When the eagle is handled at a later time, the band tells
researchers how old the eagle is and where it hatched.

*Only Native Americans are allowed to
have eagle feathers, which they use
for their ceremonies.*

The Bald Eagle Protection Act, a federal law, was created to protect eagles. It prevents eagle nest trees from being cut down or disturbed. It also makes it illegal for people to possess any part of an eagle, even feathers. By protecting eagles we are protecting a beautiful and important bird.

Other titles available in our popular

WILDLIFE *For Kids* SERIES™

Bats *For Kids*
• ISBN # 1-55971-545-6

Bears *For Kids*
• ISBN # 1-55971-134-5

Beavers *For Kids*
• ISBN # 1-55971-576-6

Bison *For Kids*
• ISBN # 1-55971-431-X

Butterflies *For Kids*
• ISBN # 1-55971-546-4

Cheetahs *For Kids*
• ISBN # 1-55971-665-7

Dolphins *For Kids*
• ISBN # 1-55971-460-3

Eagles *For Kids*
• ISBN # 1-55971-133-7

Foxes *For Kids*
• ISBN # 1-55971-637-1

Hawks *For Kids*
• ISBN # 1-55971-462-X

Kangaroos *For Kids*
• ISBN # 1-55971-595-2

Loon Magic *For Kids*
• ISBN # 1-55971-121-3

Manatees *For Kids*
• ISBN # 1-55971-539-1

Moose *For Kids*
• ISBN # 1-55971-211-2

Owls *For Kids*
• ISBN # 1-55971-475-1

Pandas *For Kids*
• ISBN # 1-55971-594-4

Raccoons *For Kids*
• ISBN # 1-55971-229-5

Sharks *For Kids*
• ISBN # 1-55971-476-X

Whales *For Kids*
• ISBN # 1-55971-125-6

Whitetails *For Kids*
• ISBN # 1-55971-122-1

Wild Horses *For Kids*
• ISBN # 1-55971-465-4

Wolves *For Kids*
• ISBN # 1-55971- 123-X

**See your nearest bookseller
or order by phone 1-800-328-3895**

NORTHWORD
NORTHWORD PRESS